A VERY

DIFFERENT

Christmas

WHAT ARE YOU

HOPING FOR

~ THIS YEAR? ~

RICO TICE

and

NATE MORGAN LOCKE

A Very Different Christmas
© Rico Tice/Nate Morgan Locke/The Good Book Company, 2015
US edition

Published by
The Good Book Company
Tel (North America): (1) 866 244 2165
Tel (UK): 0333 123 0880
International: +44 (0) 208 942 0880
Email (North America): info@thegoodbook.com
Email (UK): info@thegoodbook.co.uk

Websites
North America: www.thegoodbook.com
UK & Europe: www.thegoodbook.co.uk
Australia: www.thegoodbook.com.au
New Zealand: www.thegoodbook.co.nz

ISBN: 9781784980337

Printed and bound by CPI (UK) Ltd, Croydon, CR0 4YY
Design by André Parker

CONTENTS

For Lucy, Cat and Grace –
thank you.

According to my wife, I buy Christmas presents that are spontaneous, expensive, and not particularly useful.

I think that's her kind way of saying that my gift-buying is poorly planned, overpriced, and unhelpful. She's learned not to hope for great things when she unwraps her present from me. There's always a wry smile—or perhaps it's a resigned smile—on her face as she opens it.

There seem to be two types of people when it comes to Christmas shopping. The first type start preparing the previous June, and by October their purchases are all made. They can spend December relaxing, looking forward to Christmas, and wrapping all those thoughtful, helpful, well-priced gifts they've already bought.

The second type swear every January that they will become one of the first type, but they never do. I'm in this camp. We first start preparing—and panicking—on about 18th December, and the next week is spent racing around, hoping someone might push Christmas back a week, and buying all those spontaneous, expensive, not-particularly-useful-but-at-least-I've-got-something presents. I don't know which type you are—if the first, have pity on the rest of us, and if the second, I know your pain.

But whichever type you are, everyone knows that a big part of Christmas is the presents. It always has been, from the first time you lay awake as a child on Christmas Eve, checking the time every hour to find that in fact only two minutes had passed since you last checked. Adults always tell children that it's about the giving, not the receiving, but kids don't tend to fall for that. Then you grow up and discover that there is some joy in giving as well as receiving—and, if you're a Type Two person, you also discover that there's great relief in having found something to give.

But along with the desperate sprint around the shops to get the presents, there's also the question of where you'll open them, and who'll be there when you do. For some, Christmas is a diplomatic challenge with the potential to start a small family war. Particularly if you have children, there are too many living rooms with Christmas trees and relatives sitting around who want you to join them. You can't be everywhere at once, and so you have to remember who you were with last year, appease someone with the offer of a Thanksgiving Day visit, and hope you can avert a crisis. It's a diplomatic tangle the State Department would struggle to straighten out.

For some, though, Christmas Day isn't about panicked shopping or tricky diplomacy. It's about quiet disappointment, or even desperation. To borrow from Charles Dickens, Christmas is both the best of times and the worst of times. It's a time of joy and loneliness, of excitement and despair, often within the same family and even in the same heart.

For so many of us, there's a lot of sadness wrapped up with the tinsel each Christmas; there's grief nestled among the presents. My children will be three and five this Christmas, and there will be such joy in watching them open their presents (my wife will buy them, so they'll be well-planned, good value, and just what they want). But there will also be sadness, because my mother—who loved planning, wrapping and giving presents— was always the cornerstone of our Christmas, and she won't be there this year. So many of us, even as we open our gifts, are aware of the empty chair at the table, or are crushed because we're the only person there. For some of us, at one level we're just hoping to make it through this December.

I don't know where you'll spend Christmas Day, or who you'll spend it with. I don't know whether you're looking forward to it, or longing to get it over with. But in this book, I want you to imagine something a little weird, but something that is also wonderful. Something that can make sense of the panic, the tensions, the fun, the sadness and the joy. I want you to imagine that it's Christmas morning, and you've been invited to an amazing living room to open the presents. It's not yours, nor is it your relatives'.

It's heaven's.

As you go in, you see the tree, with the presents underneath. And in this celestial living room is you, and God. Which means that as you enter the room, there are three others already in there; because God, mysteriously, is one God and three Persons—the Father, the Son and the Holy Spirit. This view of God is hard to get your head around—but, according to the Bible, it's reality. Each of those Persons is fully God, and different from each other, and united in one God. It's what is sometimes called the Trinity.

I can't get my head round that, and I imagine you can't either—and I want to say right at the start that we never will fully comprehend this, and actually that's ok. It would be a very small, limited and slightly disappointing God whose nature our human minds could fully understand. It's exciting that God is bigger and more mysterious than any god we could imagine or make up. And this book is about that God—the God who is more interesting, wonderful, and at times challenging than the gods we dream up.

And it's with this God in his heavenly living room that you're spending Christmas Day this year. It's a very different place to visit for Christmas. There they are—the eternal, divine One Family of Father, Son and Spirit. And there are some gifts, under the tree. It turns out that Christmas, even in heaven, is all about the presents—the presents under the Trinity's tree.

This is a book about God, and you, and four gifts.

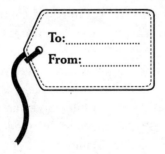

To: ....
From: ....

By the way, whenever you see "I" or "me" in this book, it always means "Rico."

THE FATHER'S GIFT

.... *Chapter Two* ....

So there you are, in heaven's living room with God on Christmas Day, and God the Father says, *Let me go first. I'm going to give my gift, and it's for...* and he looks in your direction... *you.*

And you're thinking, *Well, what's God going to give me for Christmas?! What's he got me? He's the all-powerful, all-knowing God, he can give me anything!*

IF I COULD HAVE ANYTHING...

What would you like to be given by God? If you could have anything, what would it be? The story is told of a radio-show host in Washington, D.C. who rang round some ambassadors from various countries in the run-up to Christmas one year, asking them what they would most like for Christmas.

The French ambassador was first to pick up. His answer? "Peace and goodwill to all men."

Next on the list was the Chinese ambassador. He thought for a moment and then said, "I'd like an end to hunger and disease throughout the world."

Then the radio show host called the British embassy, and was put through to the ambassador. "What would you most like for Christmas, Mr Ambassador?"

"I'd be very happy with some aftershave and a new pair of slippers."

Most of us, if we could have anything, would ask for far more than the ability to smell good and have warm feet. What would you ask for? A loved one back, to share Christmas with again? Honestly, I'd give almost anything to have my mother back with us.

Or maybe we'd be a bit more materialistic—a ten-million-dollar house would be great. Or perhaps we'd ask for the dream job. Or the dream body, or relationship, or holiday, or pension.

Perhaps, though, we should be a bit more unselfish. I mean, this is God's present to us. So he really could give us world peace. He really could end hunger and disease. Maybe that's what's in this gift that God the Father is holding out to you! So you take the present, and you start to unwrap it, and you look inside, and what is it?

A baby.

That's it? A baby? And it's not even a baby who'll live with you, but one who lived in history, 2,000 years ago. God could give you anything, and he gives you a baby? Does he know what he's doing?!

Yes, he does.

WHAT'S IN A NAME?

Here's how the Father gave the world a baby, and why this baby is special, in the words of one of the men who wrote a biography of that baby (once he'd grown up, obviously):

> *This is how the birth of Jesus the Messiah came about: his mother Mary was pledged to be married to Joseph, but before they came together, she was found to be pregnant through the Holy Spirit. Because Joseph her husband was faithful to the law, and yet did not want to expose her to public disgrace, he had in mind to divorce her quietly.*
>
> *But after he had considered this, an angel of the Lord appeared to him in a dream and said, "Joseph son of David, do not be afraid to take Mary home as your wife, because what is conceived in her is from the Holy Spirit. She will give birth to a son, and you are to give him the name Jesus, because he will save his people from their sins."*
>
> *All this took place to fulfil what the Lord had said through the prophet: "The virgin will conceive and*

give birth to a son, and they will call him Imma-
nuel" (which means "God with us").
                    (Matthew chapter 1, verses 18-23)

Did you notice the two names of the baby that
God has given as his present to the world? There's
the one we're more familiar with—Jesus—and
another that is mentioned much more rarely—
Immanuel. But we need to wrap our heads round
what Immanuel means: God with us.

When God gave us this baby, he was giving us
himself. Mary's son was not Joseph's son (that's why
he nearly divorced her)—he was God the Father's
Son. He was Immanuel—God living in this world,
God walking on the pages of human history.

WHY IMMANUEL MATTERS

This is the difference between a general experience of God, and really experiencing God. We
can sense God's divine power, if we choose to.
Have you ever stood on the shore of an ocean,
and seen its vast expanse, and watched the power
of breaking waves? Or looked up at the sky on
a clear night and been awed by the number and
magnitude of the stars and galaxies? Many of us,
when we do that, sense that the power that made
all that, if there is one, must be immense. It's a
general experience, and possibly a fleeting experience, of God.

But with the Father's gift of Immanuel—with the Son's arrival as a baby—we have received something much more precious. God identifies with us. God came to us. It's extraordinary, when you think about it. Not only did God's Son come as a person, he came as a *baby*—completely vulnerable, completely open, completely dependent. The hands that crafted the stars at the beginning of everything now reached up for a cuddle. The one who sustains the cosmos needed to be cleaned and changed. That's how God came to us, to our world—he gave himself, as a baby.

This is such great news. Why? Because Immanuel means that we can have *clarity*.

Is there a God, or gods, or nothing? What is God, or what are the gods, like? Left to ourselves, your guess is as good as mine. No one can know for sure. We have to base our lives on a guess.

Then a baby was born about whom an angel said, "What is conceived … is from the Holy Spirit." He grew up to prove by what he said and all he did that he really is God-with-us. And so the guessing games can stop. The only person who can give us clarity about the existence and character of God is… God. And God proved his existence by his appearance, and showed his character on the pages of human history. He came to a world of guessers and said, *Here I am*. If God hadn't revealed himself, to claim we can't be clear about him would be humble. Since God has revealed himself, to claim we can't be clear about him is arrogant. Immanuel gives us clarity about the big questions of life.

So for instance, Immanuel means that we know there is *eternity*. There is more to life than what we can see, and there is more to life than this life. Have you ever wondered what, if anything, lies beyond? Ever thought that there must be more to life than this? Ever grasped something that everyone said would make you happy, but the happiness faded? The atheist philosopher Jean-Paul Sartre once said:

> *"There comes a time when one asks, even of Shakespeare, even of Beethoven, 'Is that all there is?'"*

God-with-us says to us, *No, there is much, much more. You were made for eternity, and eternity is where you can find the satisfaction that eludes you now.* As C.S. Lewis, the writer of the Narnia stories who became a Christian in his thirties, wrote:

> *"Creatures are not born with desires unless satisfaction for those desires exists. A baby feels hunger: well, there is such a thing as food. A duckling wants to swim: well, there is such a thing as water. Men feel sexual desire: well, there is such a thing as sex. If I find in myself*

> *a desire which no experience in this world can*
> *satisfy, the most probable explanation is that I*
> *was made for another world."*

Next, Immanuel means we have *dignity*. Who are you? Are you anything more than the sum of your atoms, which have gathered for a blink in the great impersonal sweep of time, and which will one day disperse? Put bluntly, are you anything more than a meaningless speck, no more or less important than any other speck? Are you worth anything other than your contribution to society or your usefulness to the economy? Yes—because there is a Creator God, who visited his world as Immanuel. We each have an intrinsic value and nothing that anyone else can do to us, or that we can do to ourselves, reduces or extinguishes that value. You are precious, however you feel, whatever you do, however useful you are. Nobody is a nobody to God.

Lastly, Immanuel means we know that we are *loved*. I have a friend who, when he had just started working in London, used his salary and all his savings to fly to Australia for the weekend. By the time he'd got through airport security in Sydney, he only had five hours before he needed to check in for his return flight. Why did he make that journey? To see his girlfriend. What did all that effort say to that girl? *I love you. I care about you.* He could have sent a letter, but it would not have said as much. Instead, he gave himself. That said it all.

God's Son gave up far more, and traveled far further, than my friend—from the throne of heaven to a Middle-Eastern manger. Why make the journey? Because he loves us. He cares about us. God could have sent a letter, but it would never have said as much. He gave himself—and that says it all.

God the Father could have given you anything. What he chose to give you, me, all of us, is the most precious gift he has, and the gift we most need. He chose to give us clarity, so that we could know there is more than this life; know that we have value; and know that we are loved. God the Father has given us not a thing, but a person. He has given us his Son, as a baby.

But as you stand in God's living room, you don't have too long to think about all this. It's time to open the next present—and now it's the Son picking up a present from under the tree, ready to give it to… his Father.

To: *the world*
From: *the Father*

THE SON'S GIFT

Chapter Three

Every now and then, I hit upon the perfect gift for someone. It's so exciting (partly because it's so rare) to be able to imagine them opening it up on Christmas Day and seeing them smile. My younger son, Daniel, loves Gordon the blue train engine, from *Thomas the Tank Engine*. And I know that if he unwraps anything to do with Gordon this Christmas, it will be perfect. A Gordon-related present makes his whole body wriggle with pleasure as he realizes what he is holding in his hands.

And the question I want to ask is: what do you get God for Christmas? What would be the perfect gift for God the Father, which would make him smile with pleasure? What do you get the guy who quite literally has everything?

His Son knows. As he picks up his present for his Father, he says quietly to you, *I've got an incredible gift for my Father. He's going to love it.* And he shows you what it is, in this beautifully wrapped box. And inside the box is…

Pure goodness. A perfect life—what the Bible calls "righteousness."

That's what the Son is giving the Father. He's going to give him the life he lived as a baby, as a child, as a man. He's giving him a life of righteousness in which every moment—what he thought and said and did—pleases his Father.

HUMAN MIRRORS

This is the righteousness that God wanted from the start, from the time he first made the world and made people like you and me to enjoy living in it. When he made the first man and woman, God gave them a unique position in his creation. He made them to relate to him and to reflect him:

> God created mankind in his own image, in the image of God he created them; male and female he created them. (Genesis 1 v 27)

We're quite literally designed to be like God, to reflect him, to bear his image. That's the point of our life; that's also the way to be most satisfied in our life. We're made to be mirrors of God, to reflect his beauty and his love, his justice and his goodness, to each other and the rest of the creation.

And when Jesus lived on earth, that's the life he lived. He didn't float through life on the clouds; he experienced all that we do. He was tired, he was weak, he was hungry, he knew what it was like to be laughed at, bullied, rejected, betrayed. But at every moment he reflected God's image. At every point, he was perfectly righteous. In every second, he lived in a way that pleased his Father.

So he always obeyed the Ten Commandments. That's not easy, because, as Jesus pointed out, to truly obey them involves your thinking and feelings as well as your actions. To not murder includes not ever being selfishly angry. To not commit adultery includes not imagining it in your mind. To love others means to love your enemies. Remarkably, Jesus lived that way. His actions matched the high standards of his words; he practiced what he preached.

To give you just one example: at the moment that was in many ways the highpoint of the national public-speaking tour he went on around Israel, he spoke to huge crowds and told them, "Love your enemies." Easier said than done—but when his popularity had plummeted, his enemies had arrested him, nailed him to a cross, and stood mocking him as a failure, what did he ask his Father to do? Get rid of them? No. Get him off the cross? No. "Father, forgive them" he said. He loved his enemies.

It's worth reading a Gospel sometime—one of the four historical accounts of Jesus' life—and just appreciating the kind of person Jesus was during his time on earth. Courageous. Gentle. Compassionate. Thoughtful. Patient. Passionate. Humble. Unselfish.

In fact, when we look at Jesus, we see the kind of person we all, deep down, long to be. And that's hardly surprising, because he was a man who lived the life we were all designed to live. He reflected his Father's qualities perfectly.

PLEASED

How did the Father feel about his Son? We don't need to guess—he announced it. Right at the start of his tour, Jesus was baptized in a river…

> *And a voice from heaven said, "This is my Son, whom I love; with him I am well pleased."*
> *(Matthew 3 v 17)*

That's how the Father felt as Jesus began his time in public, his three years of proving who he was through what he taught and all he did. And then, years later, after his Son had faced opposition, disappointment, exhaustion, temptation—all the things that tend to cause us to have a meltdown or to let others down—the Father repeated his verdict as Jesus stood on the peak of a mountain with three of his closest friends:

> *A bright cloud covered them [a cloud was one of the Father's favorite ways of signifying his presence], and a voice from the cloud said, "This is my Son, whom I love; with him I am well pleased. Listen to him!" (Matthew 17 v 5)*

The Father is so pleased with his Son. He loves to see him living in just the way that he wants him to; it gives him so much joy to know the Son is always aiming to please him. This is the Son's gift to the Father—himself.

Often people make the best gifts, because what usually brings us most joy is not possessions, but a person. And what brings me most joy is to see one of my sons doing something lovely. I remember recently we went to a party at a house which they hadn't been to before, and as we stood at the front door, I saw one of them reach for the other's hand. They would face this new place together. It was an act of kindness and love, and in the middle of all the ups and downs and difficulties of parenting, it was a precious moment for me.

How did I react? I looked for someone to share the moment with, for someone to join me in smiling at them. If you're a parent, you may well recognize that impulse. And that's exactly how God the Father reacts to his Son's perfect life. This righteousness brings him such pleasure, and he wants everyone else to notice it and to praise it. Jesus…

> … *made himself nothing by taking the very nature of a servant, being made in human likeness. And being found in appearance as a man, he humbled himself by becoming obedient to death—even death on a cross!*

And how does the Father, God, respond?

> *Therefore God exalted him to the highest place and gave him the name that is above every name, that at the name of Jesus every knee should bow, in heaven and on earth and under the earth.*
>
> (Philippians 2 v 7-10)

God the Father was pleased with his Son when he was baptized… pleased with his Son as he lived… and thrilled with his Son once he'd lived, and died, and risen, and returned to his heavenly home. He exalts him. He points to him and says, *Look at him! Praise him! He's amazing!*

RIGHTEOUSNESS MATTERS

That's how much righteousness means to God. That's how much he cares about it. And that matters for us. We're all made in God's image, to relate to him and reflect his character—to live a completely righteous life. Instinctively you may hear that and say, "Look, I just don't really care about this righteousness. I'm sorry, but it just doesn't matter that much to me." To that I want to gently say, "But it matters to God."

If I lived in your house as your tenant, what you cared about as my landlord would matter. And as you live in God's world, what he cares about matters. People may not care about righteousness, but God the Father does. It's why his Son's gift is the perfect present for the guy who has everything.

Righteousness matters. And standing there in heaven's living room, you start to realize just how much it matters as the Father and Son turn toward you, and now it's your turn. The question is: what have *you* got God for Christmas?

What are *you* going to give?

To: *the Father*

From: *the Son*

We've seen that the reality at the heart of the universe is that there is a God: Father, Son and Spirit. And I've asked you to imagine standing with them on Christmas Day.

Well, it may not happen on Christmas Day, and it probably won't involve a tree, but one day you and I will actually stand in front of God—not in our imaginations, but in reality. One day, "each of us will give an account of ourselves to God" (Romans 14 v 12). And the account we give of the life we've lived will determine how we spend our future; whether or not we're going to be invited to live with God for ever, in perfection, enjoying life as the people we were designed to be and experiencing an eternity of satisfaction and fulfillment and happiness.

It's great that this day will become reality. It means that God cares about what goes on in his world. It means that the justice we all long for when we or our loved ones are hurt is on its way. We are all tenants in the world that God made, and one day the Landlord of the cosmos will ask us, *What have you done in my house? Did you keep the terms of the contract?*

Or, to put it a different way, he will ask, *What kind of life have you brought to give me?*

WHAT KIND OF LIFE?

We've already seen that Jesus can give his Father a life of perfect righteousness. The verdict on Jesus is already in—the Father says, *Son, I love you. Come on in.* But what about you and me? What will he say to us?

Now at this point, some of us panic. We look at Jesus' life, and we look at our lives, and we're very honest with ourselves; and we know that the moment when we stand before God with our eternity in the balance will be terrifying. If that's you, let me say that if you're terrified, you're halfway to being overjoyed. Why? Because, as you'll discover later in this chapter, God has done something to help you. And if you're terrified, you're ready to hear and accept what he's offering you. It's if you're complacent about the prospect of standing before God that you might be unsettled by this chapter.

Because let's face it, most of us don't react with panic. We live each day with the assumption deep down that in the end, it will all be ok. We say something like, "Ok, I don't have pure, perfect righteousness, but I do have decency. I'm not perfect—nobody's perfect—but I'm decent." As a pastor, I've taken a lot of funerals, and it's very rare that someone looks at the coffin and says, "Jim was a horrible guy." No—they say, "Jim was a good man. Jim was a great father. He had his flaws, of course he did—but he was a decent man." And what lies behind those words is this verdict: *God will accept him. God will let him in.*

When I talk to people about what they think will get them into heaven, I get all sorts of responses:

> *I'm a blood donor.*
> *I go to church—almost every week.*
> *And I give money to the church.*
> *I've been baptized and I take communion.*
> *I recycle.*
> *I'm a good wife and mother and I work hard.*
> *I pay my taxes.*

In other words, *I'm a decent person. I've lived a good life. I'm a moral person. Ok, I'm not perfect, but I'll do. Decency. That's a good enough life to give to God.*

And most people will agree with you. But I'm not going to, because God's not going to.

THE PROBLEM WITH BEING DECENT

Here's the problem with decency. It's a label that covers over a lot of less-than-decent realities.

In the way we tell the story of our life to others and to ourselves, there's often a big gap between the ideal and the real. There's a huge gap between how we like to see ourselves—and would like others to see us—and how we really are.

Did you ever read Lance Armstrong's autobiography? When he wrote it in 2000, it was bought by millions, because they loved the idea that here was a guy who, through sheer determination and courage, had first conquered cancer and then repeatedly conquered the Tour de France. He was a hero to them, and to himself.

He called his book *It's Not About The Bike*. Well, now we know—it truly wasn't about the bike, was it, Lance? It really wasn't—it was about the drugs. When the truth came out, one Australian library moved the book from the biography section to the fiction one.

Lance Armstrong had seemed the ideal man; the real Lance Armstrong was very, very different.

So be honest with yourself. Be realistic. God says that real goodness—righteousness—means you've never lied. You've never gossiped. You've never held a conversation where your sole purpose is promoting yourself, however subtly.

And this stops me in my tracks, because I do that

all the time! We all do, I think. And that desire to promote myself leads to envy of others, so that I can't just be happy when they do well. The writer Gore Vidal once said, "Whenever a friend of mine succeeds, a little something in me dies." I don't like myself for it, but I can relate to that. I love myself far more than I love others, a lot of the time.

LIFE ON FILM

Just imagine for a moment that your life was turned into a book, or better yet, a film. And it's a film that recounts everything you've ever done, said and even thought. Everything. So you get the pre-release copies delivered: *Your Life*. Maybe the strapline is: *A decent person*.

And as you put it on and watch, there's so much there that you're pleased with. You have been a good child, or spouse, or parent. You have worked hard. You have been kind. You have sacrificed your own comfort to help someone else. There is much to be pleased with, much that you could sit and watch alongside anyone and feel relaxed and confident about.

But then as you watch, you see so much that, quite frankly, you're ashamed of. The people you've made cry. The people you've trodden on to get to where you are. The people you've hurt—and some of them were people you loved. The people you could have helped but never even noticed. The selfishness. The anger. The impatience. The lust, perhaps even the physical adultery. All the things that you are so grateful that no one except you knows about.

Arthur Conan Doyle, the creator of Sherlock Holmes, once wrote as a joke to the twelve most respectable people he knew who were living in London, sending them a telegram that simply said, "Flee! All is revealed." Within 24 hours, six had left the country. I can relate to that. There is so much in my life that is not decent, let alone perfectly righteous, that I never want to be revealed.

I'm so relieved that that film of my life will never be shown in a cinema near me. So glad that no one will ever see a record of all that I've done, said and even thought.

Except that they will. "Nothing in all creation is hidden from God's sight" (Hebrews 4 v 13), including our lives; and one day, we're going to have to give an account for them.

BEAUTY AND BROKENNESS

So why are we like we are? Why is our life a mixture of the good, the bad, and the ugly—a combination of beauty and brokenness? Why is there in most of us enough good for us to be able to say we are, and think we are, decent; and yet enough bad in us that we would be horrified for that film of our lives to be shown in public?

Well, it's because we are made in God's image—made to be *like* God, capable of great good—but we're also people who are capable of great wrongs because we want to *be* God—and so we want to remake God in our own image, to fit in with our plans and preferences. The heart of the problem is the problem of our hearts. Fundamentally, we were made to say to God, "Your will be done." We are designed to say, "I'll do things your way," and enjoy living life according to the Maker's instructions. Instead, we say, "*My* will be done," and we rip up his instructions and decide to live by our own manual. And so, as Jesus himself put it:

> It is from within, out of a person's heart, that evil thoughts come—sexual immorality, theft, murder, adultery, greed, malice, deceit, lewdness, envy, slander, arrogance and folly. (Mark 7 v 21-22)

He's not saying you've done *all* those things. But he is saying that you've done *some* of those things, and will continue to do them, however hard you try not to.

A LIFE OUTSIDE

So let me take you back to heaven's living room. What are you going to give to God? Do you think that your life, as God unwraps it—as he undoes the beautifully tied bow and looks under the expensive wrapping paper—is going to please him?

Is it the kind of present that he wants? No. He is not going to look at this gift, with envy and deceit and greed and theft nestled in the box amid the kindness and thoughtfulness and generosity, and say, *You're my child. With you I am well pleased. Come in and enjoy our family Christmas, my child.*

So what do you do, as you stand in that living room in the presence of the perfect God?

You leave.

You look at Jesus, with his gift of righteousness. You look at your own gift. And you know you can't stay. This is a perfect place—and your life isn't. This is the place you were made for, the place you would love to enjoy for ever, the place that the best parts of your life in this world are mere glimmers of. But it's not a place you are able to stay in.

You're going to walk outside, before you're sent outside as the Father recoils from the "decent" life you've offered him. You're going to stand in the cold, looking in. There's God—Father, Son and Spirit—with all the angels, enjoying perfection in the warmth. And you're outside.

That's what the Bible calls hell—a real place, outside the loving presence of the loving God. A place to be endured, not enjoyed: without joy, friendship or hope. It's a place out in the cold, with only regret for company. Some people think hell is where the party is. Quite the opposite— heaven is where the party is, because it's where the God who gives us everything good will lavish his gifts on everyone who's there.

When we give an account to the perfect God who knows everything about us, there will be no welcome. We'll be shut out of the presence of the God who we chose to shut out of our lives. That's God's punishment for how we've treated him, and others, in his world. He'll give us what we've chosen, and we'll have an eternity to regret it, with no way to come inside.

Unless…

YOU DON'T NEED TO LEAVE

So you're about to leave heaven's living room. But before you reach the door, Jesus speaks to you again. He says, *I can see you're completely unprepared to stand before my Father. Listen. I'll tell you what I'll do. I've got this life of perfect righteousness to give the Father. Look at the gift tag: To Dad, from Jesus.*

And then he says something staggering: *Why don't you let me write your name on the tag alongside mine? We'll give it to him from both of us. And why don't you let me take your present and get rid of it. I'll deal with it. Just give it to me.*

And so you do. Of course you do! And you give Jesus' gift to the Father together with him, and the Father smiles at Jesus because he knows exactly what he's just done. And then he looks at you and smiles and says, *You're my child, who I love. With you I am well pleased. Enjoy the party.*

Why would Jesus do that? Very simply, because he loves you. Why would the Father allow that? Again, very simply, because he loves you:

> For God so loved the world that he gave his one and only Son, that whoever believes in him shall not perish but have eternal life. (John 3 v 16)

How can Jesus do that? Well, remember that at the first Christmas, he was given two names: Immanuel—meaning "God with us"—and Jesus. And Jesus means something, too. It means "God saves." So the angel told Joseph:

> [Mary] will give birth to a son, and you are to give him the name Jesus, because he will save his people from their sins. (Matthew 1 v 21)

Sins are what the Bible calls all the thoughts and words and actions that flow from our hearts when we refuse to say, "God, your will be done" and insist on saying, "My will be done." And Jesus was born to save us from our sins and their consequences. He was quite literally born to die.

When he died, at the end of his life of perfect righteousness, he was giving up his life to deal with our mess. As he died, he cried out, "My God, my God, why have you forsaken me?"

(Matthew 27 v 46). He knew the answer—he was being abandoned, shut out from his Father's loving presence for the first time in the whole of eternity, because of our sins. When Jesus died on a cross 2,000 years ago, he was taking our sins and dealing with them—he was experiencing his Father's displeasure and anger at our sins. He was going through hell for us.

WHAT TO DO WITH A MAGNIFYING GLASS

When I was a child, my dad's business sent him to Africa, and so the Tice family moved to Uganda. As a little boy growing up in Africa, I had two hobbies (there was no children's TV)—stamp collecting and butterflies. Both are amazing in Africa.

For both of them, you need a magnifying glass. But I soon found, as a five-year-old boy in Africa, that making stamps and butterflies bigger was not all a magnifying glass could do. I found that if you took one out into the midday sun, the possibilities were endless! You could set alight a leaf; or a piece of newspaper; or even the gardener's hut. I found that you could burn patterns onto fences and trees. Best of all, I found that if you held your sister down, you could scare the living daylights out of her! You can use a magnifying glass to focus the rays of the sun into such a sharp intensity that they burn things.

Well, imagine a massive moral magnifying glass. And through it passes not the heat of the sun's rays, but God's punishment of the selfishness, the hatred, the blasphemy, the lust, the brutality and the indifference he sees all around his world—including in my heart. Through it comes his punishment of my determination to say, "My will be done" instead of, "Your will be done", and all the hurt that this has caused to those around me.

And all that my sins deserve, and all that the world's sins deserve, was focused through this moral magnifying glass until with terrible intensity it hit one man, as he hung on a cross in first-century Palestine, and this man—God the Son—cried out in spiritual agony. At the cross, we see what we deserve. And we see that we don't need to face it.

As Jesus took his final breath, he shouted, "It is finished" (John 19 v 30). He was saying, *I've done it—I've dealt with it—I've taken the gift that you call decency but my Father calls sin, and I've dealt with it.* And then three days later, he rose from the dead to prove he really had dealt with our sins, and to offer us his perfect righteousness.

WHAT WILL YOU GIVE?

So what will you give to God? It could be your decency, your best efforts—a gift that will see you standing outside in the cold, looking in on the party, shut out for ever. Or it could be Jesus' righteousness, his perfection—a present that will please the Father, and that will mean you can enjoy life as his child, enjoying perfection for ever.

That's what you can give to the Father, because of the cross and the empty tomb. Jesus holds it out to you and says, *Write your name next to mine.*

But there's one more present under the tree. And the Holy Spirit steps forward with a smile, and comes towards you. It's for you…

To: *the Father*
From: *the Son*
and me

THE SPIRIT'S GIFT
Chapter Five

What would Christmas be without endless re-runs of famous movies? *The Wizard of Oz… Toy Story… It's a Wonderful Life… Die Hard… The Matrix…* there's everything from schmaltz to sci-fi, from films that help you sleep to films that make you think.

And the 1999 blockbuster *The Matrix* falls firm-ly into the "make you think" category, because it prompts us to ask the question: *what is reality?*

Or, to put it in the film's language:

"Do you want the blue pill, or the red pill?"

That's the choice that is offered to Neo, played by Keanu Reeves. Reeves' character has spent his whole life living in a fake world, duped by a complex computer program (the Matrix) into thinking he is free when in reality he is actually a slave. But then he is introduced to Morpheus, who offers him a great, though troubling, gift: the gift of reality.

Morpheus holds out to him a blue pill and a red pill, telling Neo:

> *"Like everyone else you were born into a prison that you cannot smell or taste or touch. A prison for your mind. You take the blue pill, you wake up in your bed and believe whatever you want to believe. You take the red pill… all I'm offering is the truth, nothing more."*

Neo takes the red pill. Which is both lucky (otherwise *The Matrix* would have been a much shorter film) and unlucky (because its success meant it became a trilogy, and the sequels were nowhere near as good).

Of course, *The Matrix* is just a film. But it raises a crucial question: is what I *think* reality is, what reality *actually* is? Am I swallowing a blue pill without even realizing it?

Let me take you back to heaven's living room. The Spirit is coming towards you with his gift.

It's reality.

That's what the Spirit offers. A view of the world as it really is, and yourself as you really are, and God as he really is.

THE SPIRIT OF CHRISTMAS

When it came to the first Christmas, what was the Spirit up to as the Father gave the world the gift of his Son, Immanuel? Let's look back at the Christmas story:

> *This is how the birth of Jesus the Messiah came about: his mother Mary was pledged to be married to Joseph, but before they came together, she was found to be pregnant through the Holy Spirit … [later on] An angel of the Lord appeared to him [Joseph] in a dream and said, "Joseph son of David, do not be afraid to take Mary home as your wife, because what is conceived in her is from the Holy Spirit. She will give birth to a son, and you are to give him the name Jesus, because he will save his people from their sins." All this took place to fulfil what the Lord had said through the prophet: "The virgin will conceive and give birth to a son, and they will call him Immanuel." (Matthew 1 v 18, 20-23)*

God the Spirit made it happen. It's mysterious—of course it is, because it's God at work in a unique way—but he was causing God the Son to be conceived in the womb of an engaged teenager in northern Israel, in a little town called Nazareth. Christmas became a reality because the Spirit worked to make it a reality.

Not only that, but the Spirit had already explained what would happen. "All this took place" according to a plan—a plan that God, "the Lord", had already made public through one of his messengers, or prophets: a man named Isaiah. Isaiah had lived in Israel seven hundred years before Mary and Joseph's lives were turned upside down by the Holy Spirit. How did he know what to say? How did he know that one day, a virgin would conceive a child and give birth to God-with-us? Because as he spoke, the Spirit guided his words:

> *No prophecy … came about by the prophet's own interpretation of things. For prophecy never had its origin in the human will, but prophets, though human, spoke from God as they were carried along by the Holy Spirit. (2 Peter 1 v 20-21)*

So as we look at the events of the first Christmas, it was the Spirit making them happen; and it was the Spirit who, hundreds of years before, had already explained their significance.

JUST A FAIRY STORY?

But—and this is big "but"—is this anything more than a fairy story? Is there really a three-in-one God? Did the Father really give the world his Son? Does he really care about righteousness? Did the Son really live a life that pleased the Father? Is our gift of "decency" really so offensive to the Father? Can we really give our mess to the Son, and be allowed to give the Father his righteousness? Maybe what you've read so far has sounded amazing to you. Maybe it's sounded offensive. But is it real?

This is where the Spirit offers you a gift right now. Reality. Here's how Immanuel, Jesus, explained what the Spirit does for people:

> *When he comes, he will convict the world of guilt in regard to sin and righteousness and judgment: in regard to sin, because [people] do not believe in me; in regard to righteousness, because I am going to the Father, where you can see me no longer; and in regard to judgment, because the prince of this world now stands condemned.*
>
> *(John 16 v 8-11, NIV84 Bible translation)*

Good friends who really love you are prepared to challenge you. If they see you going wrong, making a huge mistake, whether it's in a relationship or in your business or whatever, they will come to you and say, "Friend, this is a problem. You've got to stop." That's what the Holy Spirit does. He "convicts"—he reveals truth, even if it's deeply uncomfortable. The Spirit shows the situation to you as it really is. And he shows you three troubling, yet liberating, truths.

SIN IS DEEPER

First, he reveals that your sin is real, and that it is a huge problem. The Spirit convicts people "in regard to sin"—he shows us that sin is deeper than we ever thought. He makes us realize that sin is not naughty-but-nice, a bit of a treat, a small mistake that doesn't really matter much. He enables us to see that sin is a declaration of independence from God—pushing him from the center of our lives to its suburbs.

The ultimate yardstick of sin is this, says Jesus: that people "do not believe in me." Without the Spirit's help, we look at God the Son's birth and we see a cute story, not Immanuel coming into history; and we look at God the Son's death and we see a sad failure, not Jesus rescuing people from their sins.

I remember reading about an American who, on the night of an awful ferry disaster, risked his life time and again to dive into the water and rescue 17 people. Later, someone asked him about what stood out in his mind from that terrible night. Startlingly, his reply was:

> *"One thing stands out. Not one of those 17 people has ever written to thank me for saving their lives."*

Not one of those 17. And that just gives an inkling of what is behind Jesus' words: people "do not believe in me." Jesus didn't just risk his life. He gave it. He sacrificed himself so that men and women can have eternal life—so that we can be forgiven. So to reject him is not an intellectual exercise; it is a decision with eternal consequences. It is the heart of what sin is, and the Spirit works to show us that this is how we've been living. Maybe he's been showing this to you as you have been reading this book. Maybe he's doing it right now.

RIGHTEOUSNESS IS HIGHER

Second, the Spirit shows you that righteousness matters, and that you don't have it. Righteousness matters more to God, this world's Landlord, than we as tenants tend to appreciate; and it is a higher standard than we tend to realize. Righteousness, as we've seen, is much more than just being decent. We spend our lives bluffing, and we get very good at it. We manage to convince others that we're cleverer, funnier and better than we really are. And we manage to convince ourselves, quite a lot of the time.

But you can't bluff God—you can't convince him you're righteous when you're not. And that's what the Spirit shows us. He shows us Jesus as we read about him in the Gospels, and he shows us that this is what righteousness looks like. We begin to realize that righteousness is wonderful as we see it in Jesus. But then we look at ourselves and realize that our best deeds are nothing compared to the man we see there. Seeing the genuine article helps us identify a forgery. And as we compare ourselves with Jesus, we begin to realize we've smashed the image of God we were made to display. We begin to accept that we are not righteous.

But then the Spirit also shows us that we can have Jesus' righteousness. He shows us that it's really true that we can never develop our own righteousness and give it to God. And he also shows us that it's equally true that we don't need to, because God the Son developed righteousness in his life and death, and gives it to us. We don't have to work for acceptance from God and try to hide our flaws; we can give him our flaws, and be accepted anyway, because Jesus died for them and gives us his perfection. We can't bluff God, but we don't need to. He knows all about us, and he came and lived and died for us anyway. That's what the Spirit shows us is real. Maybe he's been doing that in you as you have been reading this book. Maybe he's doing it right now.

JUDGMENT IS CLOSER

Then third, the Spirit shows us that judgment is real, and it's close. Why? Because "the prince of this world now stands condemned." That's a way of describing the devil. There's a great line in *The Usual Suspects*:

> *"The greatest trick the devil ever pulled was convincing the world he didn't exist."*

Jesus never made that mistake. He knew the devil is real, and that his aim is to blind people to reality. The devil wants people to see Jesus as a cute story for Christmas, and to think that all mention of judgment is intolerant and unbelievable. He wants people never to realize the reality of their sin and of Jesus' righteousness. He wants people to ignore the fact that one day we will meet God not around a Christmas tree, but as he sits on his throne—and ignore the truth that he will ask us how we've lived and how we have treated his Son in our hearts.

And so the Spirit works to show people the reality. He works to enable people to suddenly stop, after years of totally ignoring the whole idea of having to give an account to God, and to say to themselves, *This is real. Judgment is real. It's going to happen to me.* Maybe he's been doing that in you as you have been reading this book. Maybe he's doing it right now.

ALL HE'S OFFERING

This is the gift the Spirit offers. Reality. Jesus promised that "the Spirit of truth … will guide you into all truth" (John 16 v 13). As the Spirit works in someone's heart, they find that Christianity is no longer a cultural expression, an outdated irrelevance, a lifestyle choice, or an emotional crutch to lean on. They find that all this begins to make sense. They realize that all this is true. Jesus becomes real. Judgment becomes real. Eternity becomes important. The offer of righteousness looks very, very precious.

All the Spirit is offering is the truth. Maybe there's a sense in you right now that you need to do something in response to what you've been reading—that's the Spirit working in you. Maybe you'll find, once you've put this book down, that you can't shake off what it said about Jesus. That'll be the Spirit working in you. Maybe you'll push this to the back of your mind and forget about it, but in a couple of years, in a moment of great joy or great difficulty, you'll suddenly remember what you read about. That'll be the Spirit working in you. He shows you reality.

That's his present, which he holds out to you.

To: *You*

From: *the Spirit*

ONE QUESTION

Chapter Six

This book is about God, you, and four presents—the Father's to you, the Son's to the Father, yours to the Father, and the Spirit's to you.

And it's about one question:

What will you do with the gifts God is offering you?

It's a question that matters more than any other. It's far more crucial than answering: what are we doing this Christmas? What will I buy this Christmas? How will I get through this Christmas?

Where you will spend this Christmas matters far less than where you will spend eternity—with God in perfection, or on your own with only regret and self-recrimination to accompany you.

So, as God holds out his presents this Christmas, will you:

Take what the Father gave you that first Christmas Day—his Son, Immanuel?

Take what the Son gives you to make you ready for your final day—perfect righteousness, as he takes your mess and gives you his life, to offer to the Father?

Take what the Spirit gives you today—reality?

These are gifts that have been eternally prepared, cost everything to offer, and will be the most precious things you can own today and for all of eternity. If you take them—if you ask the Spirit to show you in your head and your heart the reality about the Son, so that you can accept his righteousness and know his Father as your Father—then everything changes. The events of the first Christmas become the most wonderful news you have ever heard. Christmas becomes very different. In fact, life becomes very different.

You can live knowing you are forgiven—that all your regrets can go, that all your failings are wiped away. You can be honest about your sin, without being crushed by it.

You can live knowing you are loved—that your greatest successes and your worst flaws do not change one bit how loved you are by God.

You can live knowing that you are safe—that the One who made and owns this world is your

Father, who you can speak to and rely on every moment of the day.

You can live knowing that one day, when this life is over, when all your Christmases are past, and you stand before God and face the prospect of enjoying eternity with him or enduring eternity without him, you will hear the words, *Come in! You are my child, who I love. With you I am well pleased.*

And then the party starts.

To: *You?*

From: *God*

WHAT NEXT?

Thanks for reading this book—we hope you've enjoyed it and found it interesting and thought-provoking. Often when you get to the end of a book like this, it's worth asking yourself: *what next?*

We guess you're one of two "types" of people (not to be confused with the organized/disorganized gift-buying types of people we mentioned in chapter one)…

Perhaps you're someone who would like to keep looking into Christianity before you make your mind up whether you believe it's true. If that's you, we'd love you to do two things. First, read a Gospel. There are four historical accounts of Jesus' life: Matthew, Mark, Luke and John (the "Christmas story" appears in Matthew and Luke). Why not take time to read one of them and find out more about Jesus? Mark's the shortest—it takes around a couple of hours to read. Second, pray—speak to God and ask him, if he is there, to help you see the reality about who he is and who you are.

Two other things you could do: go to a website—christianityexplored.org allows you to keep thinking about Jesus in your own way, at your own pace. Or go on a course: *Christianity Explored* is an informal, seven-week walk through Mark's Gospel, where you can ask questions, discuss, or simply listen. You can find a course near you on that website we just mentioned.

Perhaps, though, you're reading this page as someone who has accepted the gifts God is offering you—you've become a Christian. If that's you, that's fantastic! Christmas, and life, will be more real and more wonderful from now on. But getting going as a Christian can be quite daunting. The best things you can do are to find a church near you that bases all it says and does on the Bible (in the same way this book does); and to start speaking to God (praying) and listening to God (reading his word, the Bible). If you'd like a hand from us with finding a church or getting started with prayer and reading the Bible, you can contact us via: info@thegoodbook.com.

Thanks again for reading.

THE FIRST CHRISTMAS
.... *by Matthew* ....

This is how the birth of Jesus the Messiah came about: his mother Mary was pledged to be married to Joseph, but before they came together, she was found to be pregnant through the Holy Spirit. ¹⁹ Because Joseph her husband was faithful to the law, and yet did not want to expose her to public disgrace, he had in mind to divorce her quietly.

²⁰ But after he had considered this, an angel of the Lord appeared to him in a dream and said, "Joseph son of David, do not be afraid to take Mary home as your wife, because what is conceived in her is from the Holy Spirit. ²¹ She will give birth to a son, and you are to give him the name Jesus, because he will save his people from their sins."

²² All this took place to fulfil what the Lord had

said through the prophet: [23] "The virgin will conceive and give birth to a son, and they will call him Immanuel" (which means "God with us").

[24] When Joseph woke up, he did what the angel of the Lord had commanded him and took Mary home as his wife. [25] But he did not consummate their marriage until she gave birth to a son. And he gave him the name Jesus.

[2:1] After Jesus was born in Bethlehem in Judea, during the time of King Herod, Magi from the east came to Jerusalem [2] and asked, "Where is the one who has been born king of the Jews? We saw his star when it rose and have come to worship him."

[3] When King Herod heard this he was disturbed, and all Jerusalem with him. [4] When he had called together all the people's chief priests and teachers of the law, he asked them where the Messiah was to be born. [5] "In Bethlehem in Judea," they replied, "for this is what the prophet has written:

[6] "'But you, Bethlehem, in the land of Judah,
    are by no means least among the rulers of
        Judah;
for out of you will come a ruler
    who will shepherd my people Israel.'"

[7] Then Herod called the Magi secretly and found out from them the exact time the star had appeared. [8] He sent them to Bethlehem and said, "Go and search carefully for the child. As soon as you

find him, report to me, so that I too may go and worship him."

[9] After they had heard the king, they went on their way, and the star they had seen when it rose went ahead of them until it stopped over the place where the child was. [10] When they saw the star, they were overjoyed. [11] On coming to the house, they saw the child with his mother Mary, and they bowed down and worshipped him. Then they opened their treasures and presented him with gifts of gold, frankincense and myrrh. [12] And having been warned in a dream not to go back to Herod, they returned to their country by another route.

Matthew 1 v 18 – 2 v 12

EVERYONE HAS A PICTURE OF JESUS.
Why not meet the real one?

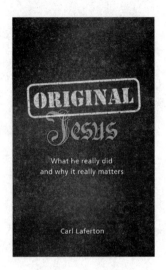

ORIGINAL JESUS
Carl Laferton

"Lively and engaging, this book makes clear who Jesus is—and why we need him. A great introduction to the true Jesus."

Gavin Peacock, ex-English Premier League Chelsea Midfield Player

thegoodbook.com/oj

the**good**book
COMPANY

Opening up the Bible

Thanks for reading this book. We hope you enjoyed it, and found it helpful.

Most people want to find answers to the big questions of life: Who are we? Why are we here? How should we live? But for many valid reasons we are often unable to find the time or the right space to think positively and carefully about them.

Perhaps you have questions that you need an answer for. Perhaps you have met Christians who have seemed unsympathetic or incomprehensible. Or maybe you are someone who has grown up believing, but need help to make things a little clearer.

At The Good Book Company, we're passionate about producing materials that help people of all ages and stages understand the heart of the Christian message, which is found in the pages of the Bible.

Whoever you are, and wherever you are at when it comes to these big questions, we hope we can help. As a publisher we want to help you look at the good book that is the Bible because we're convinced that as we meet the person who stands at its centre—Jesus Christ—we find the clearest answers to our biggest questions.

Visit our website to discover the range of books, videos and other resources we produce, or visit our partner site www.christianityexplored. org for a clear explanation of who Jesus is and why he came.

Thanks again for reading,

Your friends at The Good Book Company

NORTH AMERICA
UK & EUROPE
AUSTRALIA
NEW ZEALAND

thegoodbook.com
thegoodbook.co.uk
thegoodbook.com.au
thegoodbook.co.nz

866 244 2165
0333 123 0880
(02) 6100 4211
(+64) 3 343 2463

WWW.CHRISTIANITYEXPLORED.ORG
Our partner site is a great place for those exploring the Christian faith, with a clear explanation of the good news, powerful testimonies and answers to difficult questions.